# THE NATURE OF THINGS

*poems by*

# Tracey Daley Brocker

*Finishing Line Press*
Georgetown, Kentucky

# THE NATURE OF THINGS

Copyright © 2019 by Tracey Daley Brocker
ISBN 978-1-63534-869-9 First Edition
All rights reserved under International and Pan-American Copyright Conventions. No part of this book may be reproduced in any manner whatsoever without written permission from the publisher, except in the case of brief quotations embodied in critical articles and reviews.

## ACKNOWLEDGMENTS

Grateful acknowledgement to *Vision and Voice* published by The Joyful Jewel, Pittsboro, NC. In which these poems appeared:

"Grandpa Told Me" 2017
"The Elephant in the Room" 2018

I would like to thank my teacher, Judy Hogan, who introduced me to the world of poetry, and who constantly challenges me to take risks and cut out all unnecessary words.

Publisher: Leah Maines
Editor: Christen Kincaid
Cover Art: Tracey Daley Brocker
Author Photo: Judy Daley
Cover Design: Leah Huete

Printed in the USA on acid-free paper.
Order online: www.finishinglinepress.com
       also available on amazon.com

                Author inquiries and mail orders:
                      Finishing Line Press
                      P. O. Box 1626
                Georgetown, Kentucky 40324
                         U. S. A.

# Table of Contents

| | |
|---|---:|
| Fidelity | 1 |
| The Sea | 2 |
| My Mother | 3 |
| Conscious Conscience | 4 |
| Walks with my Grandfather | 5 |
| Bird of Prey | 6 |
| How Does My Garden Grow? | 7 |
| The Elephant in the Room | 8 |
| One less Door | 9 |
| Death Is not an Option | 10 |
| Ode to Texting | 11 |
| If I Go | 12 |
| Love Defined | 13 |
| In the Dark | 14 |
| The Funeral | 15 |
| Knowing | 17 |
| Grandpa Told Me | 18 |
| The Last Good-by | 19 |
| In Defense of Men | 20 |
| Chameleon | 21 |
| The Human Conundrum | 22 |
| Life | 23 |
| Away from the Flame | 24 |
| What's the Hurry? | 25 |
| Rain | 26 |
| You Are Not My Daddy | 27 |
| The Bridge | 28 |
| Nighttime Thoughts | 29 |
| Going Back | 30 |

*For my granddaughters, Olivia and Noelle,
who personify the beauty and wonder of nature*

**Fidelity**

The look of adoration in your eyes.
Attentiveness to my every word.
Celebration of my happiness,
sharing my pain.
Watching my movements
as if they were a performance
you don't intend to miss.
The pained expression on your face
each time we part.
The joy at my return.
Quizzical looks you give me
delving deep into the workings of my heart,
seeing my soul.
Loving what you see.
If only you were a man,
not a dog.

## The Sea

I load my brush with thalo green and ultramarine blue
to paint the sea.
It's choppy today.
I put it on thick and leave lots of brush strokes.
I lighten up the background where
the sea meets the horizon.
Waves are next.
I pause,
look at the sea,
realize my painting is a poor substitute for the soul of this place.
I can depict the surface,
but I can't unveil the secret world beneath,
teeming with life,
microscopic to monolithic.
Rip currents that in a moment
may sweep you away,
the sound of pounding waves on their way to the shore,
endless motion of the tides,
vastness,
power.
I resume painting
what I see and feel.
It isn't enough.

**My Mother**

was young when she left me.
So was I.
Friends said that I would always remember her as young
and never have to watch her fall apart with age.
That was comforting.

But she did not see me graduate from college.
She did meet the man I would marry,
but wasn't in her seat at my wedding.
She did not suffer through labor with me,
or share my joy at the birth of my son.
She was never there to answer my questions, celebrate my victories,
or assuage my defeats.
I miss her and wonder if she would be pleased with the person I have
   become.

I have inherited her dark brown eyes, sassy attitude, wicked sense of humor,
and love of dogs and nature.
When I paint, her creativity flows through my fingers and onto the canvas.
Perhaps she has been here all this time.
In me.

**Conscious Conscience**

My conscience is like chronic post nasal drip.
Nor sure where it comes from.
Possibly genetic.
It lies dormant for a bit,
lurking in the shadows.
Then, often inconveniently,
pops out with a big snuffle,
reminding me I'm less than perfect.

It seems to me some folks
simply don't have a conscience.
That little something that keeps them from living off their relatives,
or telling others just how stupid they are.
A perennial sinus headache might be useful here.

Personally, I don't mind having ethical feelings.
Though they can stifle my desire to tell a jerk how I feel.
A conscience will keep me from doing and saying the wrong thing.
Like pointing out to a friend the spider web in her fireplace.

It doesn't matter whether heredity or environment
brought on this condition.
It keeps me on my toes, so I'll tolerate it.
But you won't catch me leaving the house without a hankie.

## Walks with my Grandfather

Each afternoon we walked.
I watched our shadows,
one tall, one short.
We talked.
You taught me many things;
of nature and how to live with it,
of life and how to live it.
You spoke with a quiet strength
full of kindness, understanding, and
unconditional love.
All as tall as the shadow you cast.

Now I walk alone.
I still seek your advice.
If I listen, I hear your answer.
My shadow is somewhat taller now.
Yours, always the same.
Always there.

**Bird of Prey**

I see her often,
soaring in high, wide circles,
taking advantage of thermals and updrafts,
and watching…always watching.

It is her nature to spend her days
scavenging, usually silently,
but, with an occasional hiss or grunt,
ever on the lookout for her next victim.

She doesn't always wait for death.
An aggressive predator, she will attack the weak,
begin her picking, claim her prize.

She's a maleficent creature,
with keen sense of smell and sight.
A Jezebel, always on the fringe of life,
feasting on opportunity, creating it if possible.

She watches.
I watch…her.

## How Does My Garden Grow?

Not as well as some.
My thumbs are brown.
Though not a plant whisperer,
I sense a quivering of leaves
as I stumble past azaleas in my haste
to reach the gazebo and my wine glass.

I ponder:
To prune or not to prune?
Where?
Below the bract or above?
What the hell is a bract?

By the second glass,
I'm on to fertilizer and mulch.
Before or after the bloom?
Whose bloom?
Who blooming cares!

Then there's watering.
Temperamental Hydrangeas like their feet wet.
Crepe Myrtles get all bent out of shape
when they get soaked.
So do I.

By my third (or is it fourth) glass
it's too complicated.
I look at the garden with furrowed brow and mutter
"Grow, dammit!"

## The Elephant in the Room

He enters, his bulk swaying from side to side,
covered in the mud that is his life.
Standing solidly on four tree trunks,
he stares at me and shakes his ugly head in disbelief at my presence.
I feel defenseless, a mere ant to be crushed beneath his massive feet.

His rheumy eyes bore into mine.
Unyielding, challenging.
His dense skull is impenetrable to my feelings
as he blocks the way to entrances, exits, freedom.
The massive wrinkled body, slow with age but still determined,
moves forward placing himself between me and my dreams.

Does no one see how he bullies his way in, knocking over everything in his path?
Does no one hear him raise his head and trumpet his displeasure at my existence?
Does no one feel my pain or care when he thrusts out his trunk
demanding yet another peanut when I have nothing left to give?
Has no one noticed that even when he's not, he's always here?

**One less Door**

I could see morning as a frightening thing.
There's one less door than I had yesterday.
The clock ticks, the calendar runs away with my life.

Where has it all gone?
Opportunities missed.
Risks never taken, books never read.
Family, friends I'll never see again.

The face I see in the mirror
reveals new frailties and worn out parts.
The body I live in takes longer
to do what I used to do so effortlessly.
Why face another day?

But the day beckons and offers me another chance:
to try new things, say things left unsaid,
and learn something new even if I don't have time to use it.
Morning gives me the gift of one more door.

**Death Is not an Option**

on which I care to focus.
It is a depressing thing to think about.
How much time is left to me?
Certainly less than I had yesterday.
Will I be missed?
Who's going to take care of all the things
for which I am responsible?
I go into a tailspin when I attend
funerals of family and friends.

Where do you actually go when you die?
Don't tell me it's all heavenly,
I prefer to make my heaven right here and now.
Also, I don't want everything to be perfect.
I wouldn't have anything to fix.

Then there's judgement day.
Who set that up?
Since I'm no angel here,
I'm likely to be in trouble there…wherever there is.
Speaking of angels, I don't want to play a harp
and the prospect of seventy-nine virgins doesn't interest me.

Will I be able to see those I love?
I've never been visited by a dead person.
At least I can't prove I have.
Is there something after death, or is it the end…
I mean end, final, termination?
Oh! What If I don't like being dead?
Can I come back?
We certainly can play that the other way.

Death doesn't have much of an up-side to me.
I know it's eventually required,
but for now, since I'm able,
I'm going to pretend it doesn't exist and run out and dance in the rain.

## Ode to Texting

It's inconvenient to speak to someone,
or you simply don't want to.
Let your thumbs do the talking.
You're not eager to hear the reply,
Or you don't want your boss or co-workers
to know you're on the phone?
Let your thumbs do the talking.
It's illegal to talk and drive,
or you're in a busy restaurant?
Let your thumbs do the talking.
Texting's unlimited!
Don't want to miss your favorite program,
or you and your family are awaiting
the outcome of a dear one's surgery?
Let your thumbs do the talking.
While using your dueling digits,
it would be wise to remember:
Words are only seven per cent of a message.
There is no substitute for the tone and tempo of the human voice.
OMG doesn't count!
Feeling misunderstood?
Got fired, lost a friend,
or pissed off your wife or mother-in-law?
Could be if…
you let your thumbs do the talking.

# If I Go

by some, I won't be missed.
They will feign remorse,
but, secretly, rejoice.
I am an impediment to the life they want
and expect…
the life of more;
more money, more things,
entitlements they hold in great esteem.
They see their cushioned future
slipping away.
What they took for granted
no longer assured,
because I am here.
I sense their bitterness,
inwardly flinch at their veiled allusions.
I could stop that.
Sometimes I'd like to.
I won't because doing so would gift them with what they want…
More.

**Love Defined**

Always be there when they need you.
Listen, don't judge.
Make things about them, not you,
and give without expecting giving.
Value what…is…more than what might be.
Respond, don't react.
Don't ignore, but select.
Be willing to be vulnerable and taken for granted.
Work with what life has given.
Don't sweat the "small" stuff,
and turn loose of the need to control.
Some might consider this foolish…
I call it love.

**In the Dark**


is an unseen world full of small creatures, foraging.
Food is easier to find in the safety of the night.
Predators are there for the same reason.
If I can't see or hear this world,
how do I know it exists?

It snowed last night,
blanketing everything in a pristine powder.
As I made my way to the chicken house to release the hens
and replace frozen water, I noticed tracks everywhere.
Evidence that as I sleep, the world that seems so still,
isn't.

Rabbit tracks covered the fine dusting,
heading everywhere, some coming to an abrupt and messy end
in a flurry of owl prints.
Mice feet, barely noticeable.
Deer sign, some big and deep, others dainty,
barely marring the surface surrounding the corn
scattered the previous afternoon.
Footprints of coyotes, which I never see, only hear their chilling howls.
Possums, raccoons, both night hunters, had passed this way.
Early morning birds, seeking seeds blown in the night wind, leave
    their marks behind.
Traces of squirrels who popped out of their nests before I popped out of
    mine.

There were tracks everywhere, helter-skelter, or not.
Most I understood, some still unknown.
The night world is a busy place.
Because I can't see or hear it doesn't mean it isn't there.
Only that I am unaware.

**The Funeral**

I sit here
amid beautiful flowers,
Lifting colorful heads above green.
Cloying.
Background music,
Soft, plaintive.
Annoying.

They come in
hesitantly in black.
With soft voices
Saying:
It's for the best.
What a great guy!
He will be missed.
God, was he funny!
Remember when he…

I sit here
taking in the platitudes.
Barely breathing.
Mask in place.
Waterproof mascara,
requisite hanky, clutched tightly, black dress, pearls,
nails lightly polished.
I sit here
Thinking;

Why now? Why me?
How dare you
leave me!
How will I manage?
The children.
What do I say?
Can I give them what they need?

What would you do?
These people.
Are they mine or only yours?
Will they stay?
Did I love enough, say enough, give enough?
I wasn't finished.

I sit here
numb and full of fear.
I don't cry,
just wring the hanky.
My insides are broken.
I still don't cry.
Will they notice?
What will they think?

I sit here
Surrounded but alone.
I sit here,
but, I'm not here.

## Knowing?

I see you often.
Do I know you?
Probably not.
Like the shadows on the wall
of Plato's cave,
you are subject to interpretation.
Mine.
Viewed through my filters:
principles, experiences, personality and beliefs,
opinions are formed,
not knowledge or reason.
I can't access your thoughts or feelings.
I say "I know how you feel."
I mean I know how I'd feel.
So I study you.
Don't presume to know,
but seek to understand.

## Grandpa Told Me

one bright day at the conflux of the Deep and the Haw
the mighty eagle, Pi, was searching for a mate.
Suddenly a magnificent female appeared below.
Pi flew down in all his splendor,
screaming, squawking, blustering, generally bombasting.
You get the picture.
The transcendental fellow had a big ego.
Pi is a hard name to live up to.
The female was not impressed.
She'd heard that line before.
As she flew away, Pi, so entranced by the sun glistening on
her white tail feathers, crashed right into the big birch at the river's edge.
Now, that hurt.
Gone was all that raucous bravado.
He began to whimper
as men will do.
The female heard his plaintive, sweet call
and flew to his side to console him.
Women are suckers for men in distress.
To this day you can see them on a winter's morning,
fishing the Haw and calling to each other
in cheerful, lively tones.
According to Grandpa Aesop,
Pi learned it's wiser to chirp than to squawk.

**The Last Good-by**

We sit side by side,
my best friend and I,
in the station awaiting the train
that will take her far away.

I will miss her but will remember and savor this day
as we talk of the past, silly moments we've shared;
feats and foibles of our children, each of us one boy,
one girl, now grown with children of their own.
Projects, adventures, dreams.
Creativity that magically appeared
when we put our hearts and minds together.

It's time for boarding,
for one last hug that says so much
but not enough.
She pauses on the top step, turns and smiles at me.
I smile back.
Inside, I crumble.
Suddenly I'm angry, incensed
at all that is being taken from me
by this train to nowhere…
The Alzheimer's Express.

**In Defense of Men**

Men are expected to:

Grow up, get married, have a family, take care of them forever and like it.
Open doors.
Understand women.
Be stronger, work harder, never give up, and always put family first.
Pick up the tab.
Take out the garbage.

Don't even look at other women. Oh, wait! You can look but not too long and don't touch!
Remember, women can dress provocatively…don't respond!
Put the seat down.
Man up.
Be more sensitive. Is this an oxymoron?

Don't think women suffer from penis envy.
Where to keep it? Will it go up, stay up, long enough or too long?
Who wants to worry about that?
Look, I don't think men are perfect.
Lord knows they have many flaws.
But in the words of Gelett Burgess…
"I'd rather see than be one."

## Chameleon

Little loden creature,
how long have you been perched
on the back of my green rocker,
staring at me,
daring me to notice?
I move.
You move,
to the table beside me,
and turn brown!
How clever of you.
Sheer genius to blend in wherever you are.
You go unobserved, yet see and hear everything.
I know people like you.
Some are Geminis.
Some are hypocrites.
A few, like you,
have an uncanny ability to make where they are
who they are.

## The Human Conundrum

is being right.
Rightness is our heritage,
what we are taught from birth.
Our need for rightness shapes us,
causes us to shower grace upon those who agree with us,
curry no favor with those who do not.
We human beings condemn, vilify, ignore,
or actively pursue the downfall of those
whose choices are not ones we'd make.

Is this noble?
If I wish you harm,
celebrate your blunders,
or judge you as less,
am I truly more?

**Life**

Each day is an adventure.
Choices are made:
how my time will be spent,
what decisions will I make?

I can plan, stay with the plan,
or choose something new...
lots of somethings.

I can respond rather than react,
turn lemons into lemonade,
or discover that the hard things
are not so hard.

I can find a bright spot,
sit in it, mull over who I am
and who I want to become.

Life is about challenge.
The beginning is the beginning.
The end is the end.
Everything in the middle is
uncharted territory.
I love that.

**Away from the Flame**

As I enter the room,
I am drawn to an inviting warmth
like a fly to honey.
I move closer.
The welcome seems friendly,
but somewhat false.
A screen warns me to keep my distance.
All is not as it seems.
Sudden crackles and pops
presage an unforgiving nature.
Ashes float as visible remains of the
destruction of an inner core
too hot for comfort.
I turn my back.
You are too forbidding to face.

## What's the Hurry?

Why rush to the finish line?
Why hurry through everything when the end comes way too soon
and sometimes sooner?
We take pride in our children who crawl, talk and walk before their peers,
and spout "grow up, act your age, and big boys don't cry."
Why push our children to hurry up and grow up?
What's wrong with savoring the fleeting moments of childhood?

We can hardly wait to drive or be twenty-one
with all the privileges and responsibilities of being "grown up."
We hurry to appointments booked too close together
and strive to find the perfect job we can remain in till we retire to count
    our grey hairs.
We live on "Someday Isle" waiting for our ship to come in
so we can pursue those passions we put on hold.

Shouldn't we make the most of our moments,
living each stage as if it were the only one we would ever see?
Why come to the end before we appreciate the beginning and the middle?

**Rain**

Rain comes at night.
A torrent, drenching everything in its path.
A kettle drumming force of nature.
Like the mighty Moldau
it rages and sweeps away care and imperfection,
erasing, purifying in the deep, heavy tones of oboe and cello.
Building to a thunderous crescendo it collapses upon itself.
Then descending, flowing gently but with intention, like strings.
Morning brings awakening of new life.
Something small uncurls,
coaxed to the surface by lilting gentle rain.
The sun teases the new bud to spread its petals in its own song.

**You Are Not My Daddy**

I already have one.
Why do I get punished when I can't call you that word?
Like the time I was sent to my room cause I couldn't say,
"Please pass the potatoes,
Daddy."
Don't know why you and Mommy won't let me call you something else.
It would be easier.

I feel like I disappoint you.
Math is easy for you,
I'm pretty terrible at it.
You don't understand why
so you make me work extra hard.
I guess you think I'm stupid.
I make As in everything else,
but that's not good enough.
You never spank me,
I'm afraid you might, so I try hard
not to make you mad.

I want you to like me.
I kinda like you.
You are not mine.
I am not yours.
My last name is different.
I think everything would be better if it wasn't.

## The Bridge

I am the bridge
that takes you from where you are
to that place you want to reach.
How do you see me?
Long? Short? High and humpbacked?
Strong and unyielding steel and concrete?
Or wood, flexible, vibrating under your weight,
clickety clacking as you cross?

What kind of bridge do you need?
Do you approach quickly with a sense of purpose,
or take a deep breath and utter a prayer
as you begin your passage?
Are you unwilling to cross because you are afraid of bridges,
or accepting of any bridge that gets you to your objective?

Once committed, what do you do?
Dangle a line over the side and hope for a bite?
Toss in a pebble and contemplate the widening ripples?
Have an insane desire to climb the side and plunge into the depths below?
Do you amble across, marveling at the shape of clouds and the lapping
    water,
or run like hell in fear of the eighteen wheeler bearing down on you?
Am I the way you choose to go, a pleasant diversion, or a general nuisance?
Is it important what a bridge is,
or simply that there is one?

## Nighttime Thoughts

As I slumber in the arms of Morpheus
you come to me,
unbidden, but not unwelcome.
You are doing what those close to you remember most…
playing your signature drum solo from
"The House of the Rising Sun."
The sultry sounds tease my imagination
as I watch you, in your own dreamland,
captivated by the beat.

I see your face frozen in irrepressible laughter
at one of the many ridiculous pranks you pulled
or a joke you told for the umpteenth time.
I watch you attend a wedding dressed in bib overalls and carrying a shotgun.
I catch a view of you strolling down the street
in your three-piece, pin-striped suit, wing tips and a propeller-topped beanie.

How joyful, full of life and your mischievous self!
Your presence is as overwhelming as it has always been.
As delightful images of you float through my mind.
I find myself lost in the land of Hypnos,
as the dream weaver presents our play of love remembered.

## Going Back

It's been said you can't go home again.
It won't be as you remember and you will be disappointed.
Some years ago I was drawn to a place
I hadn't seen in fifty years.
An imposing white building surrounded by mossy tipped oaks,
stood in the park of my childhood.
I walked through the doors, noting the lofty ceiling, stacks everywhere,
long tables, whispers, and subdued lighting.
I turned right and headed down the marble stairs to the basement,
the place where my quest for knowing began.
It all returned.
Overwhelmed by the sight, sound, and smell of all those books,
I was once again in my childhood's favorite place.
Memories of hours cherished here filled my senses.
It was as if I had never left.
Though many things change as we grow older,
some places, like the Willowbranch library,
still have the power to stir your imagination and touch your heart.

Tracey Daley Brocker describes herself as an introvert, comfortable in her own skin and plagued with an insatiable need to understand the motivations of the people around her.

The experiences of higher education, marriage, raising a son and daughter, and spending a large part of her adult life working as a communications consultant taught her the importance of understanding and propelled her to try to write in a more accessible language.

Having grown up with the notion that if it didn't rhyme it wasn't poetry, she finds free verse...freeing. Mostly because it allows her to write the way she thinks...in short bursts with fewer adjectives. She hopes this style makes her message clearer to the reader.

# The Joshua Poems